Make a splash: Create a pond

Contents

Water has a special magic, provides a constantly changing focus in the garden, and adds to a feeling of calm. For the natural gardener it performs an invaluable function, enticing a whole range of useful birds, insects and other wildlife. If the idea of a water feature is appealing, however, the result often isn't: poor planning and maintenance can land you with a green, stagnant bog. This book gives you clear, concise advice on how to plan, build and maintain a pond in even the most modest garden – and without spending a fortune.

1

Creating a new pond

Planning

Location, location, location

One of the key decisions you will have to make is where exactly to put the pond. In a small garden options may be limited, but give some thought to how large the pond will be, how deep it will be and how much sun it will get. A small shallow pond in constant full sunlight will quickly become too warm and rapid evaporation may mean you will have to keep topping the water up. A pond with too many overhanging trees and bushes will accumulate rotting fallen leaves that encourage bacteria, which then deplete the oxygen in the water and create a thick smelly ooze at the bottom.

The best situation is one with an open sunny aspect on the southern side, not overhung by trees or bushes, but with a hedge or a fence near enough to offer some shelter from severe weather without producing too much shade.

Note: a small hollow or depression that is already wet and marshy may not be the best place to put a pond as it will already have its own special and interesting plants and animals.

A bigger pond will support more wildlife. Above, a pair of Azure damselflies Coenagrion puella *meet at the pond margin.*

Bigger is better

The bigger the pond, the better it will be at attracting wildlife and maintaining a balanced ecological mix. A large pond with **at least one deep area** will be well buffered against the extremes of heat and cold that our climate throws at us. Shallow water can become too warm in summer, as a consequence it carries less dissolved oxygen and encourages the growth of stifling blanket weed algae. Even if a pond ices over during winter, deeper water will still be several degrees above freezing point.

Linings

There are **four basic types** of pond lining and which one you choose will depend on how big your pond will be and the geology of your local soil.

- **Pre-formed fibreglass** or plastic liners come in a variety of standard shapes and relatively small sizes. They are cheap and easy, but they look less natural because their sides are often too steep to get good naturalistic plant cover.

- **Concrete** needs to be waterproofed and a wire mesh to support it and to prevent it cracking. It needs to be laid quickly and skilfully in good weather. It is prone to weather damage and repairs can be awkward. Its true place is in public spaces where its vandal-proof properties outweigh its ugly appearance.

- **Puddled clay** is the most traditional means of pond construction. Naturally underlying clay, or clay brought in specially for the job, needs to be softly trampled into a thick smooth layer that lines the pond excavations. It is really only suitable if the pond is dug in an area with a high water table which will naturally fill the pond when it is dug. If an old pond is to be revived, re-puddling the existing clay may be the best thing to do.

- **Rubber and plastic liners** are easy to install, but care has to be taken not to puncture them. Polythene is the cheapest, but it is thin, fragile and deteriorates quickest; several layers are needed to give at least a few years life-time to a pond. PVC liners are a little more expensive; at 0.5mm thick they are still rather thin and fragile, but usually have a 10-year guarantee. Butyl rubber liners are the most expensive, but are generally regarded as the best choice. They are thicker (0.75mm) and tougher and often come with a 20-year guarantee. Very large ponds may need the thickest and strongest, 1mm, butyl liner; it is relatively cheaper than the standard gauge, but is less flexible and more difficult to work with.

The wide availability of these modern sheet liners makes them the best choice for almost all ponds and it is this means of construction that will be emphasized here.

Design

It's all a matter of personal taste and your design can be whatever you choose. Think about how it will fit with the rest of the garden. Will it be formal with straight lines? Will it be irregular and naturalistic? Will it have any other 'hard' landscape features such as paving or decking around its edges?

One of the most important practical aspects of design is considering what you will do with all the earth you remove.

Don't think that by only digging a shallow pond you will get rid of the problem. It's important to have some deeper parts (at least 60cm) so that plants and animals have some protection against too warm water in summer and freezing conditions in winter.

Often, the dug soil can be used to correct any slope at the pond site, or to make an embankment around part of the edge of the pond.

action stations

1 **Location:** Choose a situation with an open sunny aspect on the southern side, not overhung by trees or bushes. A hedge or a fence nearby will offer some shelter without producing too much shade.

2 **Size:** The bigger the pond, the better it will be at attracting wildlife and maintaining a balanced ecological mix. Ensure you have various shelf depths and at least one deep area.

3 **Design:** It's all a matter of personal taste and your design can be whatever you choose. Think about how it will fit with the rest of the garden. Will it be formal with straight lines? Will it be irregular and naturalistic?

4 **Liner:** Rubber and plastic liners are easy to install and relatively cheap. However, consider the options and decide what is right for you – alternatives include pre-formed fibre-glass, concrete or puddled clay.

2

Building your pond

The common toad Bufo bufo sheltering in the shallow pond margin.

Excavation

First mark out the outline shape of the pond. Use a rope, a hose-pipe
or dry sand poured out of a bottle to mark the shape. If you are at all unsure
about the design, leave the outline in place for a few days until you get used
to it or decide to change it. How does it look from different angles or from
an upstairs window? An oval or kidney shape is an easy and attractive
starting point.

Most small garden ponds can be dug by hand but if you are feeling
ambitious and have the space for a larger pool, you might hire a mechanical
digger for the day. If you do, make sure the machine you hire has the
necessary access to and around the site.

Giving your pond **the edge**

It is important to have all the edges of the pond at the same level, otherwise areas of bare liner will ruin the illusion of a natural pool. Peg-out the pond boundaries at roughly one metre intervals and level them using spirit level and a plank of wood. As you dig the hole use the spoil to make an even and level pond margin.

The edges of the pond can be shelved to allow different water depths for different plants and should have gentle slopes to allow aquatic animals to crawl in and out easily.

If you want a natural transition from pond to garden, rather than a formal paved edge, surround the pond embankment with a narrow ditch all around; this will be where stones and soil can be laid to anchor the pond liner invisibly in place.

Laying down the liner

If the pond liner becomes punctured, the water will drain away and all your hard work will amount to nothing but a smelly bog. The main danger is not sharp sticks being poked into it from above by inquisitive children, but the weight of water pushing it down onto sharp stones beneath. When the hole is dug and shaped, but the ground is still very stony, you may need to shovel in a layer of sand as a cushion. If the ground is not stoney and looks relatively smooth, you will still need a layer of soft protective matting. This fibre matting acts just like underlay and is usually available from the same suppliers as the liner itself. You can use old carpet (but not foam-rubber backed), and make absolutely sure that ALL carpet nails have been removed. The matting needs to cover the hole, right up to and above the projected waterline of the finished pool.

How big will my liner have to be?

Liners come in various sizes and you can calculate how big a sheet you need from the design you have created. The sheet length needs to be the proposed pond length plus twice the proposed depth. Its width needs to be the pond width plus twice the depth. This will allow you adequate extra around the edges to secure the liner with stones once it is in place.

Laying the liner down is a delicate business. Gather it into pleats or folds to fit it into any tight corners. If your pond is large and you need to get in it to move the liner about, take off your shoes and walk in socks or barefoot to prevent holing the sheet. Don't worry about firming the liner snugly into every cranny and irregularity, the water weight will stretch it to fit.

How to calculate the size of your pond liner

It's simple once you know how:

Double the depth and add to both the other measurements.

Example:

For a pond that will be 3 metres x 2 metres and 0.6 metres deep.

Liner length = (0.6 x 2) + 3 = 1.2 + 3 = 4.2m long

Liner width = (0.6 x 2) + 2 = 1.2 + 2 = 3.2m wide

And an example for those using imperial measurements:

Liner length = (2 x 2) + 10 = 4 + 10 = 14ft long

Liner width = (2 x 2) + 7 = 4 + 7 = 11ft wide

Solid **alternative**

Very small gardens might be better suited to a pre-cast fibreglass or solid plastic pond. These come in various shapes and sizes and are a good cheap alternative if space is tight. After digging the hole slightly overlarge, line it to the right contours with enough sand to cushion the fibreglass shell.

Small gardens

Even the smallest gardens can house a water-filled half barrel or butt. Water evaporates faster so topping up regularly is important. Plants can be lowered to the correct depth and suspended by wires from the top. They may be less frog- and toad-friendly, but insects including dragonflies will still visit.

A raised pond made from railway sleepers provides its own waterside seating too. Peg or bolt them together, overlapping the ends, into a triangle or square, three or four sleepers high. Dig a deep end, into the ground and use the spoil to sculpt sloping and stepped sides. After filling, the edges of the liner need to be tacked into place and can be hidden by nailing a decorative border of thick rope along the rim.

The **exciting** bit

Now is the time to fill the pond with water before you trim any liner edges. Natural ponds are fed by rain water, and although this is the best quality, tap water is perfectly adequate. Chlorine in the tap water will have gone after only 48 hours, so wait a couple of days before you start planting or introducing wildlife.

Once the pond is full and the liner fully stretched to its permanent position, you can now anchor it all around with paving slabs or stones. When the edges are secured, you can trim off the excess from the liner sheet and conceal the edges with pebbles, soil or boulders.

The arrival of wildlife to a newly dug pond may start within hours.

action stations

1 **Excavation:** mark out the outline shape of the pond. **Don't forget a deep area** of at least 60cms (24ins) to protect against extremes of heat and cold.

2 **Protect the liner:** Shovel in sand to provide a cushion and add an underlay layer of soft protective fibre matting.

3 **Pond edge:** Keep the edges of the pond at the same level. Use the spoil to make an even and level pond margin and to cover the liner.

4 **Shelve the edges** of the pond to allow different water depths for different plants and to allow aquatic animals to crawl in and out easily.

5 **Liner size, remember**: Double the depth and add to both the other measurements.

6 **Filling with water:** If you use tap water wait 48 hours before starting any planting. Trim and conceal the liner once the site has settled.

Planting

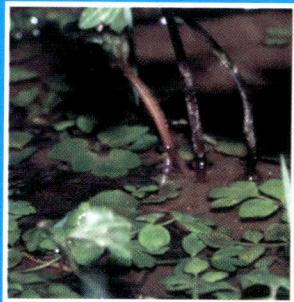

Planting your pond

Pond plants fit roughly into three broad categories (submerged, floating and marginal) and you will need some of each to make your pond as wildlife-friendly as possible. **Native species are ideal** because they are already acclimatized and are less likely to become invasive.

Most large garden centres have aquatic sections, or seek out specialist nurseries. Plant in early spring or autumn.

Submerged plants

Submerged plants live completely underwater, although they may send out their flowers to break the surface. They oxygenate the water and provide hiding places for small creatures. Native plants suitable for garden pond include:

- **water starwort** *Callitriche stagnalis*

- **hornwort** *Ceratophylum demersum*

- **water milfoil** *Myriophyllum spicatum*

- **curly pondweed** *Potamogeton crispus*

There are also many non-native plants, including: **Canadian pondweed** (*Elodea canadensis*) which does not need to be planted and can simply be dropped into the deep water.

Floating plants

Floating plants have leaves that sit on the water surface and provide shade and shelter for aquatic animals. Useful natives include:

- **waterlilies yellow** *Nuphar lutea* and white *Nymphaea alba*

- **water soldier** *Stratiotes aloides*

- **arrowhead** *Sagittaria sagittifolia*

- **broad-leaf pondweed** *Potamogeton natans*

- **water crowfoot** *Ranunculus aquatilis*

There are also many exotic water lilies available with different-sized leaves for smaller or larger ponds. **Amphibius bistort** *Polygonum amphibium* is especially useful; as well as a floating-leaved form is also has an erect form for the margins and boggy areas.

Dropping in and spreading out

The easiest way to introduce plants into the water is to pot them into mesh baskets filled with soil and compost. A large stone at the bottom will help steady the plant and a covering of gravel over the top will help keep the compost in place as you gently lower the basket into the correct place in the pond. Hold the basket just below the water surface until all the air has bubbled out, then lower to the final depth. Until the plants become completely established, you will be able to move the baskets about, to accommodate plant growth and if you want to add new plants in between.

A good rule of thumb when planting up a small to medium-sized garden pond is to **aim for about two-thirds plant cover and one-third open water**. This gives a good balance of shade and shelter to the animal life below the surface.

Marginal plants

Marginal plants grow around the shallow edges of the pond and out into any surrounding boggy areas. Ranging from low squat forms to tall erect stems, they take the eye from the still flatness of the water up into the height of the surrounding herbs and shrubs. They act like ladders for dragonfly and mayfly nymphs to climb up when it is time for the adult insects to emerge. Many native plants are available, including:

- **water mint** *Mentha aquatica*
- **yellow flag iris** *Iris pseudacorus*
- **water plantain** *Alisma plantago-aquatica*,
- **brooklime** *Veronica beccabunga*
- **flowering rush** *Butomus umbellatus*
- **greater spearwort** *Ranunculus lingua*
- **reedmace** *Typha latifolia*

Out and about

The pond habitat does not stop at the water's edge and how you finish off the margins will determine how easy it is for animals to get in and out of the water. A small froglet making its first tentative hops onto the land, or a dragonfly nymph hauling itself up an emerging stem ready for adult flight, are at their most vulnerable just as they leave the water.

Rather than surround the pond with mown lawn, leave at least some areas of the nearby garden to grow thick and tall, to blend with the emergent stems in the shallows. Better still, create a boggy area where the underlying pond liner is buried beneath the soil making a waterlogged patch. This makes a perfectly smooth transition between the deep water of the pond and dry land above. Edging parts of the pond with some boulders or logs will also provide useful hibernating sites for frogs, toads and newts. Nearby compost bins may also be

Your pond should have gentle slopes, shelves and shallows to allow aquatic animals to crawl in and out easily.

invaded by overwintering grass-snakes, secretive and harmless. In summer take care when mowing nearby lawns since frogs and toads wander far and can become victims to the lawnmower.

If your pond is more formal in design, perhaps with straight wooden or concrete edges or with a walkway and decking, it is more important than ever that there should be ways in and out for small creatures. Stepped shallows can be created by submerging several bricks in the corners and the baskets then lowered onto these shelves. A knot of variously sized pots and containers near the edge will provide some shelter for recently emerged amphibians.

Edging parts of the pond with boulders or logs will provide useful hibernating sites for frogs, toads and newts. Nearby compost bins may also be invaded by the harmless overwintering grass-snake.

Going **green**

The arrival of wildlife to a newly dug pond may start within hours, maybe just as the first water is trickling into the new liner. Flying water beetles, boatmen, skaters and dragonflies are attracted by the reflections on the water and soon arrive to investigate.

action stations

1 **Plant native species** because they are already acclimatized and are less likely to become invasive. Provide a mixture of submerged, floating and marginal plants to make your pond as wildlife-friendly as possible.

2 **Avoid invasive species** and if you do use exotics find out about them from your supplier before purchasing.

3 **Plant cover:** To provide a good balance of shade and shelter for a small to medium-sized garden pond, aim for approximately two-thirds plant cover to one-third open water.

4 **Buffer:** Leave at least some areas of the nearby garden to grow thick and tall, to blend with the emergent stems in the shallows.

5 **Bog:** Create a boggy area where the underlying pond liner is buried beneath the soil making a waterlogged patch.

Problems & maintenance tips

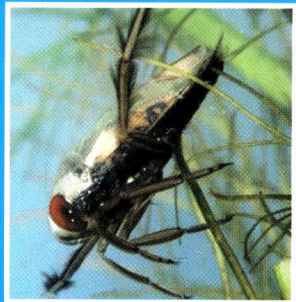

Problem **ponds**

Pea **soup?**

You might find that the first thing your new pond does is turn into a green soup. This is the natural '**blooming**' of minute green algae. It **will clear** as small creatures arrive to eat it, but you can speed up the process by introducing water fleas (*Daphnia* species). These tiny (1-2 mm) crustaceans are common in mature ponds, and can be seen flitting about a few centimetres below the surface, especially in bright sunlight. Inoculate your water with a bucket or two scooped from a friend's already established pond.

No natural pond has the crystal clear water of a swimming pool. **Slightly green or brown water is perfectly normal** and a sign that a balanced ecosystem is developing.

Asking friends and neighbours for help is often the best way to get a pond ecosystem up and running. They will occasionally need to thin-out plants that you can then use and there is always enough frog and toad spawn to go round. However, check that what you take is native and non-invasive and take note, you must get permission from the landowner before you start taking plants from ponds and lakes in the countryside.

Keep a lookout for invasive plants such as New Zealand pygmywort (above) which can quickly smother your pond and choke other plants.

Problem **plants**

There are a small number of invasive plants that you will have to keep an eye out for. Unfortunately they can be inadvertantly introduced in tiny amounts, but then become quickly established.

Most duck weeds *Lemna* species are a natural and native part of the pond flora, but they can carpet the surface, blocking out the light. **Use a kitchen sieve to scoop them out when they get too dominant.**

Water fern *Azolla filiculoides* is a tiny North American plant, **free floating with small tendril roots**. Under a hand lens it is very pretty, but it can soon smother the pond surface, choking other plants with its thick red carpet-like growth. **Remove it at all costs,** but do not dump it into the wild, where it is already an invasive pest.

New Zealand pygmywort *Crassula helmsii* forms low cushion-shaped blobs around the margins which will soon become one solid mass of dense leaves. **Avoid it and whatever you do don't let it escape into natural ponds** and streams.

Fishy **friends or enemies?**

If you create a garden pond for wildlife, DO NOT stock it with fish. Despite their attractive colours and the interest of their movement in the water, fish will soon strip a pond of all other life. Even tiny native fish such as sticklebacks are fierce hunters and will eat insects and amphibian eggs.

If you want a fish pond limit them to one fish per $2m^2$ of surface and none in any pond under 2m x 4m. If you have a very large wildlife pond, you may be able to stock it with native fish, but you must get written permission (and advice) from the Environment Agency (see page 47) – they are charged with preventing the spread of fish diseases.

The letter of the **law**

Do not put non-native amphibians or reptiles into any pond, it is unethical and illegal. In the past, several 'pet' species have become established in the wild, including the African clawed toad *Xenopus laevis* and the red-eared terrapin *Trachemys scripta-elegans*.

It is also illegal to catch or disturb our rarer species including natterjack toads *Bufo calamita* and great crested newts *Triturus cristatus*.

Rarer species including the natterjack toad and great crested newt (below) should not be caught or disturbed. If you should be so lucky as to find one, report it to your local Wildlife Trust or to Froglife (see page 48).

Maintenance tips

Most small ponds require little maintenance, perhaps clearing out thick growth of blanket weed or duckweed, or replenishing the water lilies. Large ponds may become gradually overgrown or invasive plants can edge out your carefully created mix. If you need to do major clearing, do it piecemeal, clearing alternate banks in alternate years.

When to act

Most animals are inactive during the winter, so the best time for least disturbance is **late October to January**.

Rampant pond plants

If you have to clear out burgeoning plant growth, **never remove more than one-quarter at a time,** otherwise the changes to light, oxygen levels and shelter will be too great for wildlife sheltering within. Leave dredgings on the pond banks for a day or two so creatures can return to the water.

Clearing out leaves and reducing silt

Clear out fallen leaves regularly to prevent the build up of silt. If you ever need to drain the pond for repair or desilting, translocate plants and animals into a neighbour's pond. If the liner is to be exposed for any length of time cover it with a protective layer of sand which can easily be removed before refilling.

Controlling algae with straw or hay – myth or fact?

If you have already inoculated your pond with a community of algae-consuming water fleas (see page 32) and your water still resembles pea soup, try adding straw (*not hay*) to your water. As the straw decomposes it releases an algal inhibitor which helps prevent growth of algal blooms. **Barley straw** seems to work the best and is both cheap and pond-friendly.

But don't just throw in a whole bale, the average garden pond requires just a small net of loosely-packed barley straw (appox. 50 grams per square metre of surface water). The process is more efficient when the water is well oxygenated so, a pump, fountain or regular agitation of the water will help, also try to keep the straw near the surface. For larger ponds you might try adding a little lavender straw (which will require more oxygen).

Ask for advice about straw at your local aquatic or garden centre. In addition, Rothamsted Research provide information sheets on problem aquatic plants, for a full list go to: www.rothamsted.bbsrc.ac.uk/pie/JonathanGrp/JonathanInformationSheets.html

Water level

Top up water during hot weather: smaller ponds lose water by evaporation quicker than large ponds. Add **tap water little and often** rather than in one large flood, so that changes in water temperature and chlorine have little effect. If the pond **freezes** over during winter, try to keep some areas open by breaking up the ice or rest a bowl of hot water to melt a hole.

Pests and diseases

In the last few years a mysterious **red leg disease has been killing urban frogs.** The cause is unknown and not much can be done, but report it to your local Wildlife Trust or Froglife (see page 48) so they can monitor its spread.

The appearance of a heron might at first delight, but then infuriate when it starts eating fish, tadpoles and frogs. A bird-scarer will deter other species and defeat the object of having a wildlife pond, but if you can **get the balance of plant cover right**, you will provide plenty of shelter for the pondlife to avoid visiting predators.

Cats will sometimes play with frogs, but these amphibians are remarkably resilient animals. If you should find one in the home or at the mercy of a cat, release them back into the pond, a logpile, or long grass, making sure the cat does not watch what you are doing!

Plenty of shelter in and around your pond will help to minimize any losses due to visiting predators.

Water features can present a danger to young children who should always be supervised in any garden with a pond. Additionally, a pond can be fenced off and child-proof gates installed.

Safety

Even the smallest of garden water features represent a danger to young children and although drownings are thankfully very uncommon, there are a few tragedies each year. **Children should always be supervised in any garden with a pond**. If in doubt, fence off a pond and make any gate child-proof.

Water features like butts, half-barrels and some ponds can have metal or plastic grills fitted just over or just under the water surface. Wildlife can still get in and out and plants can grow through.

action stations

1 **Allow water to clear naturally** don't be alarmed if your water turns green – this is the natural '**blooming**' of minute green algae. It **will clear** as small creatures arrive to eat it.

2 **Inoculate** your water with a bucket or two scooped from a friend's already established pond.

3 **Free plants:** If you take plants from already established ponds, check that what you take is native and non-invasive.

4 **Floating weed:** Use a kitchen sieve to scoop duck weeds *Lemna* species out when they get too dominant.

5 **Fish:** If you want a garden pond for wildlife, don't stock it with fish – they will eat everything else.

6 **Topping up:** Keep a check on the water level in your pond. Add tap water little and often to minimize the effect temperature change and chlorine.

7 **Freezing:** Keep some areas of your pond open by breaking up ice.

4

Pondlife guide

Common frog *Rana temporaria*
(top). Up to 10cm, colour varies, mottled greens and browns, dark eye patch, smooth skin, long jumping hind legs. Spawn (egg masses) in February/March, black tadpoles later become mottled brown.

Common toad *Bufo bufo* (see page 14). Up to 13cm, dark brown, sometimes lighter, warty skin, shorter walking legs. Double spawn strings in March/April, tadpoles (corruption of 'toadpoles') black.

Palmate newt *Triturus helveticus*
(middle). Similar to smooth newt, but without spotted throat, males have smaller crest, but webbed hind feet during breeding season.

Smooth newt *Triturus vulgaris*
(bottom). Usually 8-10cm, brown with yellow/orange belly and spotted throat, males with wavy crest on back and tail during breeding season (March-May).

Black water beetle *Agabus biguttatus* (not shown). Up to 11 mm, shiny black. Fast swimmer, many other species 3-20mm, some mottled or vaguely patterned.

Great diving beetle *Dytiscus marginalis* (top). Up to 33mm, yellow margined, female upperside grooved, male smooth. Dives quickly, large jaws and can bite.

Water boatman *Notonecta glauca* (not shown). Up to 15mm, distinguished by long middle legs that 'row' like oars. Dives rapidly. Several similar species.

Water scorpion *Nepa cinerea* (middle) Up to 24mm, brown, 'pincers' are front legs used for catching prey, long tail is breathing tube. Slow moving in submerged plants.

Water skater *Gerris species.* (bottom). Up to 14mm, long middle and hind legs rest on surface tension, front legs hold small prey. Very fast on water surface, several similar species.

Azure damselfly *Coenagrion puella* (see page 7). Wingspan 45mm, males blue and black, females greenish, distinctive U-shaped black mark at base of tail.

Blue-tailed damselfly *Ischnura elegans* (top). Wingspan 45mm, thorax blue, pink, purple or green. Flies in amongst reeds and rushes.

Common red damselfly *Pyrrhosoma nymphula* (not shown). Wingspan 45mm, black and red markings vary in extent. Perches on waterside plants.

Common darter *Sympetrum striolatum* (middle). Wingspan 60mm, male red, female yellow brown. Perches on nearby stems.

Migrant hawker *Aeshna mixta* (bottom). Wingspan 90mm, distinctive pale mark, shaped like a golf tee, at base of tail.

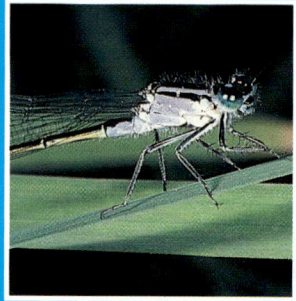

Brown hawker *Aeshna grandis* (not shown). Wingspan 100mm, largest UK species, unmistakeable brown wings. Often flies far from water.

Giant ramshorn snail *Planorbis corneus* (top). Up to 30mm diameter, soft body very small compared to shell which is shaped like a rams horn.

Great pond snail *Limnaea stagnalis* (middle). Up to 50mm long, floats underneath surface and on floating leaves.

Water hoglouse *Asellus* species (bottom). Up to 13mm, dark brown, like a woodlouse (to which it is related). Crawling in murk at bottom of pond and usually a sign that the pond is heavily silted.